POETRY FOR PARENTS

BY
LAUREN O'GRADY

Dedication

To Saul,

Here is a book, to sit on your shelf,
to some day take down and read to yourself.
You see books never die and words never age;
They get frozen in time entrapped on the page.
So these words that I write will always live on,
To remind you, 'I love you' even after I'm gone.
So turn over the page and start having a look,
This is for you, Son, your very own book!

Love always
Mum xxx

ACKNOWLEDGEMENTS

I started out writing these poems as a hobby until the people around me encouraged me to compile a book. After months of doubt and non-commitment, I finaly thought "Hey, why the hell not?" At the very worst, I will have a book to pass onto my children and somewhere that all my poems are held, or hopefully others might read these, enjoy them and maybe, hopefully, be a little happier because of them.

So, here I go, writing my acknowledgements (I think that is what you are meant to do when you put together a book). So, under the pretence that I know what I am doing as a 'proper writer' I am about to give it a go.

Saul, my gorgeous, clever, little man. In the whole two and a half years of your life, you have managed to tip ours upside down. Along with feeling incompetent and guilty at times, I have never experienced so much unconditional love and pride in my entire life. You are our world and the inspiration behind this book – although if you ever get a sibling, don't tell them that!

Brian, my equally gorgeous and clever, big man! You are the most caring and beautiful individual I have ever met. You are not only the best husband and father in the world, but my best friend and soulmate! Whatever life throws at us, we will handle it together!

Mum and Dad, I am who I am today because of you! Your selfless, unconditional love knows no bounds. I can hand on heart, say that I could not imagine better parents/grandparents than you. You have been a shining example of what it means to be great parents, great partners and just overall great people! I love you with all of my heart and could never repay everything you have done for me. – Here, have a book!

My big brothers, P.R and Lee - you guys are O.K, I guess. For fighting with me, and fighting for me, I will love you guys forever!

For everything you have done for me throughout my life and in the years to come, I will always be greatful.

My gorgeous nieces and nephew, Ellie, Keira, Isla, Cammy and the little'un on the way – may you always grow up knowing how loved, amazing and unstoppable you are!

Hayley, Helen and Kirsty! You guys are my 'Wolf Pack'! The best friends and best support group any girl could ever have! It's not where you go in life that matters, it's who is standing beside you! We always were, and forever will be an unbreakable team!

Sharon, the big sister I never had and one of the most gorgeous humans I know, inside and out! Your friendship, love and support means the world to me.

My first fans and best friends: Aunty Katrina, Tanya and Nicola. Without you guys, I would not even be writing this book! You had faith in me and encouraged me to take on this project from the start. So, here I am now, pretending I know what to write in this section of the book! Thank you, for everything!

My proof readers Nicola, Angela and Kieran, for reeding over all my wurk and insuring this book had no miscakes. Well dun!

TABLE OF CONTENTS

DUE DATE

What's the deal with due dates? Why's everyone in such a hurry?

You'll come out when you are ready; there's really no need to worry!

Some babies grow quicker than others; you'll be out in your own time.

"Yes, I know I'm still pregnant, Jean!" but I assure you we're both doing fine!

I think it's just conversational but as soon as I started to show,

Strangers would smile sympathetically, and ask, "How long have you still got to go?"

What a peculiar question! Do they understand parenthood at all?

"At least another 18 years Dave, I'm kinda in this for the long hall!"

I obviously can't wait to meet you, I feel that needs to be said.

But, what difference will a few more days make, when we have our whole lives ahead.

Now, I know we are getting nearer, to what they told me was your 'due date',

But take your time, my darling. I know you will be worth the wait.

I C ARRIED Y OU

When you love someone you carry them.
I carried you from the start;
I kept you safe and warm
in the space beneath my heart.
I carried you in a woven wrap,
I carried you from the car.
I carried you on my shoulders,
when your legs couldn't walk that far.
I'll carry you through the tough times,
when you're not feeling brave.
I'll carry you all your life,
Until you carry me to the grave!

NUMB

When they first placed him in her arms, all she felt was numb.
No rush of unconditional love, they'd promised her would come.
She tried to force affection, but her heart was cold as stone.
She was surrounded by so many, yet had never felt so alone.
She tried to force herself to feel, to force herself to care.
She thought the world would be better off, if she wasn't there.
Her spark had been extinguished, her body felt like lead.
Her energy spent fighting, the battles inside her head.
The thoughts told her she's useless, she can't do anything right.
They consumed her throughout the day, and kept her up at night.
She was incarcerated in her mind, a solitary prison cell.
Banging on the bars, for someone to save her from this hell.
No one knew how much she struggled, just to stay afloat.
The world just sailed on by, in the comfort of their boat.

BREASTFEEDING

If feeding my child offends you, please look the other way!
I absolutely will not cover up or put my breasts away.
I don't care if you think it's disgusting; I'm afraid that's your own issue.
It's just another part of my body, a nipple stuck onto some tissue.
What did you think they were for? These lumps stuck onto my chest.
They're not here to hear your opinions, or to make me look good in a vest.
I will feed my child when she's hungry; I don't care if you think me overt.
It's not my fault I'm distracting your husband, it's him who's the pervert!
I'm building my child's immune system, to help her fight off disease.
No, I won't go somewhere more private; I'll feed her wherever I please!
You don't think it's appropriate when you're sitting here with your son.
Would you rather he had the impression that breasts are just for fun?
I hope that you feel much better, now that you've said your bit.
But, if you don't mind, we're at our lunch; and you're just being a tit!

FOR MANCHESTER

Dear little man, I hold so dear,
Here is some advice
The word we live is a wondrous place,
but sometimes it's not nice!
You'll hear some things that shock you,
and make you downright sad.
The world has so much good in it,
don't focus on the bad!

Don't let it change your spirit!
Be kind and strong and brave!
Don't let evil get the upper hand,
Or the attention that it craves!

You ask if super heroes
are alive and really true,
The answer is – yes, my son,
They live inside of you;
And in ordinary people,
and in ordinary tasks,
You see little acts of kindness
don't need capes and masks!

Don't let media corrupt you,
to believe evil is a race!
Evil is a mindset!
It doesn't have a face!
It's not a specific religion.
Or a certain colour of skin.
It is a tainted, ugly darkness,
that comes from deep within.

You cannot run away from it,
no matter where you roam.
Evil's a million miles away,
But it's also close to home.
In times of tragic incidents,
when evil is unfurled
You'll see more love and compassion
than evil in this world.

It doesn't make it any better,
It's sick and bad and wrong!
So, sometimes you just need to
Pray and just keep strong!
Protect those more vulnerable,
always stand for what is right!
Follow your moral compass,
and don't be afraid to fight!
Don't let fear control you!
Take risks and always smile!
It's quality, not quantity
that will make your life worthwhile.
The road's not always easy
so remember when you're crying,
failure and mistakes
just mean that you are trying!

The world owes you NOTHING
Don't ever be in doubt.
Always put in double
than what you will take out!
The little can make a big difference;
Spread love wherever you go!
Even from the smallest acorn,
a mighty tree will grow!

So when you're faced with evil,
be sure and do all you can!
Don't cower away in fear;
stand with your fellow man!
I can't promise you an easy road,
But I promise you'll do just fine!
If it wasn't for all the darkness,
the stars would never shine!!

WE NAILED PARENTHOOD TODAY!

We were deep inside the forest, building a secret den.
We were up and out the house, before it had reached ten.
You had porridge for breakfast, followed by some fruit.
I remembered to pack your wellies, and your puddle suit.
We've collected fallen leaves, and made mud pies,
Sorted out our sticks, in order of their size.
It's time for a picnic, we sit down by a hedge.
I bring out the hummus and fresh, organic veg.
We go on a bear hunt, as we make our way back.
You spotted some footprints; we followed the strange track.
We didn't find a bear, but we still had fun looking.
At home the house is tidy, and the roast's been slowly cooking.
We play a little more, until daddy gets in.
Then he asks if we fancy going for a family swim.
After we had our swim, we head straight to the park,
Then back home for our dinner, before it gets too dark.
We all read together, then both kiss you goodnight.
We tell each other 'I love you' then turn out the light.
As we tiptoe out your room, I turn to daddy and I say...
"We totally nailed parenthood today!"

THAT GIRL I USED TO KNOW

I once knew a girl, who looked a lot like me.
She was impulsive, independent and totally care-free.
She came and she went, as quick as a breeze.
She did what she liked, whenever she pleased.
She'd say what she meant and meant what she'd say.
She'd stay out all night, and sleep in all day.
She had no restrictions, made last minute plans.
Had the world at her feet, and her dreams in her hands.
She wanted to travel, she had itchy feet
She had places to go and people to meet.
She had no worries and her cares; they were few.
I often think fondly of that girl I once knew!

So, if you ever see a girl, who looks a lot like me;
Tell her I am more than I ever dreamed I'd be!
Tell her I am busy, and no longer alone,
I'm no longer selfish, and my time is not my own.
Tell her I am happy and that my life is good!
That I wouldn't trade places, even if I could.
But tell her I still miss her, and the way we used to be,
When we were so impulsive, independent and care-free.

THE UNINVITED GUEST

You're wearing week-old jammies
A mile away from looking your best.
You hear a chap at the door...
The uninvited guest!

Your world goes in slow motion,
You can feel your rising stress.
The house looks like a bomb site,
And your child is in a mess.

I hope they haven't seen me,
You wait and hold your breath.
You contemplate ignoring it
Or faking your own death.

You think of a good excuse,
Sorry we missed you, we were out for the day
But your little human starts shouting for you
And gives the game away!

What if they think you are lazy?
That you must have just got up!
What if they want a coffee?
You'll need to find a clean cup!

You glance quickly in the mirror,
To try and sort out your hair
Is that jam from Wednesday's breakfast?
How did that get there?

You open the front door with caution,
Heart pounding and weak at the knees
"Good morning ma'am, here is your parcel"
"Can you sign this please?"

THE BITE

It's not something I had prepared for.
So, it caught me kind of off-guard,
When the phone call came from the nursery
To tell me something has just occurred.

I dropped everything and rushed over;
I knew that it wouldn't be good.
And when I got to the reception,
My sheepish little man stood.

I scooped him up into my arms,
My heart thumping, head running wild.
I was told there had been an 'incident'
Involving another child.

I couldn't see the victim,
My eyes scanned the whole place
Then paused on the red-headed girl
With teeth marks etched into her face.

Just then, an angry woman
comes barging through the door.
I presume it's 'bite marks' mother,
As she flies across the floor.

She starts shouting in my face
And points to the little girl's cheek,
Then starts shouting at my son,
Who only turned one last week.

I apologised profusely,
I said I am so sorry about your daughter,
But if you scream in his face one more time,
I'll drown you in that water.

I'm happy to discuss this as adults,
But your temper's getting out of hand.
I'll then drag your lifeless body,
And bury it in the sand.

I explained that he's only a baby,
And is finding nursery tough.
I told her that I would speak to him.
She told me,'that's not good enough'!

I told her I would explain, again,
That biting isn't kind.
She told me if he was hers,
He would have a raw behind.

I disagreed with her 'discipline',
But I decided not to say.
I figured she couldn't be reasoned with
And had suffered enough from today.

See, I don't see how hitting a child
Shows them that violence is not O.K,
It just seems counterproductive,
And probably not the best way.

And I know it's a petty victory,
But, as I was putting 'Hannibal' back in his chair,
I turned to see her little 'precious',
Grab another child by the hair.

The mum looked around embarrassed,
She didn't quite know what to say.
I just smiled and said 'kids will be kids'
Then turned around and walked away.

THE NET

There once was a young girl on the net,
Who befriended people she'd never met.
She would often boast
Of the likes on her post,
But this was something she soon came to regret.

She met a young lad called, Dean
Who told her she was the prettiest girl he'd seen!
His words, they were slick,
So, she fell in love quick
And was the happiest she'd ever been.

He was gorgeous and free of all flaws
But was too shy to meet the in-laws.
But Dean, he was fly,
As this was a lie
And he was not who he told her he was.

She loved how Dean made her smile
But behind his doctored profile
Sat an old man
With a sinister plan
Who was also a registered paedophile!

He had swept her right off her feet
Then told her a time and a street
With a smile on her face,
She went to that place
And he was the last person she'd ever meet.

THE SAME

They say everybody is different;
We are individual and unique,
But I know if I pierced your skin,
It's the same red blood that would seep.

People have different beliefs
They're as diverse as our colour of skin.
But when you strip away our shell,
We all are the same, deep within.

I know that our morals may differ
But it's the same air that we all breathe.
Our same hearts get broken and shattered,
When someone we love has to leave.

We all feel the same kind of emotions;
We just display them in a different way.
Our actions differ under pressure
But, we all feel, at the end of the day.

So, don't let your uniqueness mislead you
Into thinking that you're any better.
If we both jumped into the water,
Neither one of us would emerge any wetter.

The people we love might be different
But we love them with the same kind of heart.
And if we both stood under an x-ray machine,
You'd be hard pushed to tell us apart.

We all scream when we are frightened
When we cry, we make the same kind of sound.
We all enter the world in a similar way,
Then turn to dust as we return to the ground.

THE UNEXPECTED

There are some things I expect in life, that come as no surprise,
Like a dip in the market, when house prices start to rise.
Or, traffic at a standstill because of heavy snow.
The government breaking promises, they made not long ago.
Not getting a signal, at midnight on New Year,
Or stalling under pressure, because I'm still in second gear.
But it's the unexpected things, that catch me right off-guard,
That bring me to my knees, that hit me really hard.
Like tiny little clothes, hung up with such great care,
The tiny little clothes, that you'll never get to wear.
Or your first scan picture, that was the screensaver on my phone,
Reminding me of a baby, I didn't get to bring home.
Or how I cry at the package, the midwife gave me for free,
And its tiny little samples that were marked 'For Mums to Be'
Or the sadness that engulfs me when I walk into your room,
That makes my hand shoot up, protectively, to my empty womb.
Yes some things I expect in life, I can even see their cause.
But I never foresaw this 'mum to be' as a mum that never was.

THIS IS FOR MY PARENTS

This is for my parents, who've always been my crutch.
Who often went without, so I could have too much.
Who looked after and protected me, every single day,
Whose unfaltering love and guidance, made me who I am today.

This is for my parents. I hope you realise,
I've loved you all my life, since I opened up my eyes.
You are my inspiration, each and every day.
If I am half the parent you've both been, then I know I'll be O.K!

This is for my parents, who I could never reimburse.
Who taught me actions are worth more, than the pennies in your purse.
So, I guess I'm saying "Thank You!", for everything you do
Because all of me, owes all I am, because of both of you!

DAISY

It was a rare and magic moment,
Our son asleep in bed.
Neither of us were sleeping
And she's not got a 'sore head'.

She tapped the bed and winked,
Gave me the look – you know the kind.
So, I tore off all my clothes,
Before she changed her mind.

I knew just what she wanted;
She was trying to seduce.
But as I went to grab her breasts,
I was squirted with boob juice!

She must have got a fright,
As she let out a cry,
I couldn't stop myself from laughing
As I wiped milk from my eye.

She quickly got embarrassed.
She was blushing now.
Don't worry love, I don't mind.
You're like a little cow!

I don't know what I said wrong
But, she didn't look impressed.
She shot right up out the bed
And started getting dressed.

I thought that I was funny,
But it seemed to drive her crazy
I'd MOO when she came in a room
Or, smile and call her 'Daisy'.

I thought she'd loosen up
But she got her maddest yet.
When she told me she was feeling sick
So, I said I'd call the vet.

LITTLE FIGHTER

You came into our life a lot earlier than expected.
Now you have two birthdays as one of them is corrected.
Despite your dramatic entrance and your complicated start,
What you lacked in size, you made up for in heart.
We worried that your body might struggle to cope,
But the warrior inside you never gave up hope!
So, go forth little fighter, the world waits for you.
There's nothing life can throw your way that you can't make it through.

WOLF PACK

Every parent needs: a support group; people that have got your back.
People that stand beside you; your very own human wolf pack.
A pack that supports and encourages when you feel like you're losing the fight,
When you're ready to throw in the towel, or run away into the night.
When other people might stand and judge you, but you know for certain they won't.
When they all believe you can do it, even in the times that you don't.
They are always on hand to listen, and come baring chocolate and wine,
And after an hour of complaining, you realise that everything's fine.
Your hunting grounds may have changed; you've traded in drinking and clubs
For a night sitting in, in your jammies, watching cartoons with the cubs.
So when you feel you're alone on your journey, don't forget to look back.
The strength of the pack is the wolf, and the strength of the wolf is her pack.

YOU WEREN'T THERE

His first words, his first steps.
His first gummsy little smile.
He'll soon grow, before you know,
He's only a baby for a while.

How his giggles are infectious
As he splashes in the bath.
The little things he'll do, for only you,
Just to make you laugh.

Appreciate his cuddles,
As he snuggles up under your chin.
Memorise his smell, because time will tell,
You'll get out what you put in.

So put in the time and effort,
Build the bond while he is still small,
Because time will fly by, in the blink of an eye
And he won't know you at all.

So don't wait until he is older,
To show him that you really care,
Because if you wait, it will be too late.
And he'll no longer need you there!

He has so much love already,
So your absence won't make him sad,
It's you who'll regret, on that I can bet.
He won't miss what he's never had!

For Old Father Time doesn't pause,
His winds of change keep a blowin'.
And in a glance, you'll have missed your chance
and he'll be fully grown.

So make your choices carefully,
Because when all is said and done,
Don't accept the praise, you didn't raise
The gentleman he's become.

LISTEN WITH YOUR EYES

I'm sorry I behaved that way
I didn't have a choice!
I tried to make you understand.
My actions are my voice!

So when I drop this, you pick it up?
Great! I love this game!
Hey, why'd you take that off me?
Do you not feel the same?

That cereal was yummy,
But I can't eat any more.
Don't worry, I'll get rid of it!
I'll feed it to the floor!

Don't put that nappy on me,
My bits need to be free!
You would feel the same,
If you had to sit in your own pee!

If you stop just for a moment,
It should come as no surprise;
You'd understand me perfectly,
If you listened with your eyes.

I love it when you stroke my face,
I'll show you, just like this...
I bet you'll love it even more,
If I do it with my fist.

I drew you a beautiful picture
You'll be so proud of me!
I even used your lipstick,
Look, mum! Come and see!

I don't think that you like it.
You don't seem proud at all.
Not even when I improvised,
And drew it on the wall.

If you stop just for a moment,
It should come as no surprise,
You'd understand me perfectly,
If you listened with your eyes.

I'm sorry I threw that tantrum,
I didn't mean to strop.
I didn't' know how to tell you,
I didn't like that shop!

I wasn't allowed to touch things,
I was strapped down in that chair.
I wanted out to help you.
I didn't find it fair!

Why are we here again, mum?
I've got so many clothes.
Why are you picking up nappies?
You know my thoughts on those!!

If you stop just for a moment,
It should come as no surprise,
You'd understand me perfectly,
If you listened with your eyes.

Who's that hairy stranger?
That's saying "We've all been there!"
If that really is the case old man,
Then get me out this chair!

Oh great! Here comes another one,
Trying to talk to me!
If you're not here to help me, love
Then please just let me be!

"Someone's not very happy!"
She says, wiping away a tear.
You should be a detective, Susan!
You're in the wrong career!

If you stop just for a moment,
It should come as no surprise,
You'd understand me perfectly,
If you listened with your eyes.

Finally! We're leaving now!
Let me on my feet!
But, you take me straight to the car,
And in ANOTHER seat!

I hold my body rigid,
I scream 'til my throat's sore.
Why is no one listening?
I just can't take much more!

Now we're home from the shops,
It must be time to play.
But again you are 'too busy'
As you put the food away!

I start to cry and raise my arms.
I'm trying to make you see,
Mum, I'm really struggling here!
Please just cuddle me!

If you stop just for a moment,
It should come as no surprise,
You'd understand me perfectly,
If you listened with your eyes.

I'm still upset when dad gets home,
But as I try and say,
You sigh and pass me to him, saying
"He's been like this all day!"

I'm not trying to be difficult,
I hate when you're unhappy.
Dad asks if I'm hungry,
And if you changed my nappy?

I'm so glad that you're home Dad,
Now, won't you come and play?
You tell me 'in a minute,'
You've had a busy day.

If you stop just for a moment,
It should come as no surprise,
You'd understand me perfectly,
If you listened with your eyes.

This makes me really sad.
How can I make you see?
Maybe if I throw my toys at you,
You'll come and play with me.

You shout at me to stop it,
You tell me that I'm bad!
I tried getting your attention,
But, instead, I made you mad!

You never did come play with me,
So I just played all alone.
Instead, you drank your coffee,
And were never off your phone.

If you stop just for a moment,
It should come as no surprise,
You'd understand me perfectly,
If you listened with your eyes.

And all too soon it's bedtime,
My tummy fills with dread.
It's not that I hate sleeping,
I just can't stand my bed!

You tell me that I'm big now,
And should sleep in my own room,
But it feels like only yesterday,
I was safe inside your womb!

You try and lay me down,
I hold on as tight as I can.
I'm not trying to manipulate,
There is no master plan.

I just get really lonely
When I wake up in the night.
It's dark and full of noises,
That give me such a fright!

You and dad have each other,
To stop you getting cold.
But I lie awake shivering,
With no one there to hold.

I know you tuck me in,
And give me my teddy bear.
But it's not the same as your body heat,
Or when I nuzzle into your hair.

I used to try and tell you,
I'd cry 'til I couldn't breathe.
You'd just tell me "It's bed time!"
Then turn around and leave!

Now I do not bother,
not because I'm no longer pained,
I know you'll never listen,
So, I guess that's me 'Sleep trained'.

If you stop just for a moment,
It should come as no surprise,
You'd understand me perfectly,
If you listened with your eyes.

YOU'LL ALWAYS BE OUR BABY

You'll always be my baby, even in years to come.
You'll always be my baby, and I'll always be your mum.
You'll always be his baby, through the good times and the bad,
You'll always be his baby, and he'll always be your dad.
You'll always be our baby, no matter what you do,
You'll always be our baby, and we'll never stop loving you!

DARLING, YOU ARE GLOWING

She waddles into the room,
She struggles to get into the seat.
It looks like 'Good Year' and 'Michelin'
Have sponsored both her feet.

The sweat is pouring off her,
The extra weight is showing.
"Do I look O.K in this?"
I said, "Darling, you are glowing!"

She's on her second tub of ice-cream
She has another craving.
I look down at her legs.
I see she's given up on shaving.

She asked me if I still fancied her,
Even though she was a mess.
I told her,"no matter what you look like
I'd never love you any less!"

Her complexion is looking oily
As is the hair stuck to her head.
I told her, "I love you more than ever!"
And I meant every word I said!

IF MY LOVE

If my love could make you brave, you would never have to fear.
If my love could make you happy, you would never cry a tear.
If my love could make you rich, you would be a billionaire.
If my love could bring you comfort, you would always know I care.
If my love could always guide you, you would never go off track.
If my love could always protect you, you'd never have to watch your back.
But even love has its limits, as I have come to see.
If my love was enough to save you, then you would still be here with me.

LOST PROPERTY

She got up in the morning,
Her mum was still drunk from last night.
The electricity wasn't topped up
So she got ready without any light.

She put on a wrinkly, old vest,
She would cover with her stained blouse
She wanted to brush her teeth
But there's no toothpaste in the house.

She went in to wake up her brother;
Then they tiptoed on their tiny feet
To go downstairs and look in the cupboards
to see if there was anything to eat.

She knew even before they got there
That each cupboard would be as bare as the last
And, if they wanted to make it to school on time
Then they had to get ready, and fast!

She looked at her little brother
who was pale and painfully thin
Then as he went to put on his shoes
She had another check in the bin.

There were some leftover chips from Friday
So she quickly put them on a plate
Her brother smiled and went to share them
But she said "it's O.K, I already ate!"

They started walking quickly;
It was a mile to the nearest town
They didn't own a jacket
And the rain was pouring down.

When she finally got into the classroom,
The rain was running off her nose
The teacher sent her to the janitor
To get a dry set of clothes

The Janitor said "good to see you!
Come and take a seat!"
And before he looked in the lost property,
Gave her a breakfast bar to eat.

She wondered very briefly,
but didn't really care
Why he brought in so many bars
As they were always going spare.

She loved coming to school;
It was a safe place to be.
The teacher always listened to her
And the lunch was always free.

The dinner ladies were lovely,
They always gave her a warm smile
But they weren't very good at portions,
As she always got more on her pile.

She loved it when it was playtime,
She could run around being free and wild.
It was the best part of her day, pretending
That she was just a normal child.

And before she even realises,
It's 3 o'clock again.
She looks out of the window
and frowns when she sees the rain.

But, as she's getting ready,
While she's packing up her bag,
Her teacher pulls out a winter coat
And discreetly removes the tag.

"This was in the lost property,
It will just end up in the bin.
It's your size, you should keep it,
since you didn't bring one in!"

Then, when she went to collect her brother,
She just couldn't believe her eyes.
It turns out there was another lost jacket
and in just her brother's size!

RUSSIAN DOLL

Don't you think it's amazing,
That while I was still in your tummy;
My ovaries contained the eggs
That I used to become a mummy.
So I wonder if you realised
Or if you even knew.
You weren't just carrying your daughter
But part of your grandchildren too.

LOOKING BACK

He looked back on his life, as he neared the end of the line,
And realised he had regrets, about how he'd spent his time.
He looked around at his family, standing by his hospital bed,
And wished he could go back, and spend more time with them instead.
Like the extra days spent working, to buy that flash new phone,
leaving his wife and kids, to eat dinner on their own.
Or how he missed his daughter's starring role in the play,
Because he wanted that new car, and did overtime that day.
Or when he went to a leaving night, for a guy he hardly knew;
He missed his son's parents' night, and football tournament too.
And it started to sink in, as he looked at his kids and wife,
That he had missed so many of the milestones in their life.
Now, all that overworking, for belongings and for wealth,
Couldn't buy back the lost years and had chipped away at his health.
But he took some comfort knowing, as their eyes stung red with tears,
They'd be just fine without him, they've been practising it for years.

I FAILED PARENTHOOD TODAY!

I'm feeling rather sick. The rain is pouring down.
We've not got out our jammies, or our dressing gown.
I lie limp on the couch as I splutter and cough.
I'd have made you some cereal, but the milk has gone off.
The house is in a tip; you can't see past the clutter.
I decide to make you toast, topped with peanut butter.
I just don't have the energy to get on the floor and play.
I try to get your buy-in by saying it's a 'Duvet Day'.
We sit on the couch, watching the T.V.
Then you ask hopefully, "Will you play with me?"
I told you that I can't, I'm not feeling very well.
My heart almost broke, as your little face fell.
I put out some sweets, then start to feel dizzy.
You're probably not hungry, but I'm trying to keep you busy.
Daddy comes in from work, and kisses you on the head.
Looks at me sympathetically, and says "Get up to your bed!"
I let out a sigh of relief, then turn around and say...
"Babe, I am sorry, I failed at parenthood today!"
He put his arms around me, laughed and gave me a kiss.
He said "Parenting is made up of days just like this!"

I'M TRYING

You didn't sleep very well last night. You were up nearly every hour.
I'm trying to be a great mum today, please God give me the power!
You launch your milky cereal straight across the floor.
It's not even 9am and I don't know if I can take much more.
You're crying for no reason, as I rack my brains to think.
I have cuddled you and fed you, and you've had enough to drink.
I bring you out and cuddle you, but you just hit me away.
I'm trying son, I really am, to be a good mum today.
I try and change your clothes, you fight me in your vest.
Maybe you're still tired and need a bit more rest.
I try and lay you down, I stroke your little face.
You kick and nip and bite, and scream down the whole place.
Maybe you are bored. I take you out to play.
I'm trying son, I really am, to be a mum today.
You don't want in my arms or to walk or sit in your pram,
You're not leaving me with many options, I'm trying son, I am.
Just as I feel like giving up, you reach up and give me a kiss.
And all the struggles seem worth it, for moments just like this.
Some days I am invincible, others I break down crying.
There might never be the perfect mum, but I promise I won't stop
trying.

MEMORIES

I watch you sleeping peacefully, in the comfort of your cot.
I once was your whole universe, but since then you've forgot.
You missed me for a while, you cried and called my name,
But now you think your mummy is just a picture in a frame.
Once we were inseparable, a duo, me and you!
We'd take our naps together, between playing 'peek a boo'.
I'd blow raspberries on your belly, just to hear you laugh.
Chase you across the bed, still naked from your bath.
I still remember your smell, as you'd curl up on my chest
Or the way you'd fight and struggle, when I'd put on your vest.
I was fluent in your language, I could decipher every cry.
When you were tired or just hungry or didn't want to say goodbye.
I'm thankful for your resilience, but I couldn't help feeling sad,
When you finally stopped shouting 'Mummy' and changed your cry to 'Dad'.
I miss you both so much, and I'm sorry I'm not there,
You've had to learn so early, that sometimes life's not fair.
And it's a bitter sweet consolation, that you lost me while still so small,
As all the memories, I'll never forget, you won't remember at all.

SUPERHERO

He had heard of superheroes, and loved everything they did,
He wanted to be one of them, but he was just a kid.
How they saved the world from bad guys, and flew across the sky,
But he'd not long been walking, so definitely couldn't fly.

He marvels at their costumes, strength and lightening pace,
Then looked down at his pull-ups and a frown came over his face.
He'd seen them fly above the world, where the people looked like ants,
but he'd never seen an episode, where Batman peed his pants.

They fight against all odds and still come out the winner.
But at the moment he's just focusing, on finishing all his dinner.
He went to bed upset, realising it's sad but true,
He'd never be a hero, so just a boy would do.

He thought of all his heroes, about Ironman and Hulk,
As he hugged his teddy tighter and finished off his milk.
But fear not my little man, because if you only knew,
That when you close your eyes at night, you have super powers too!

For as you lie all tucked up, with your favourite toy,
You're transforming from a baby, into a little boy!
You see, the Flash is overrated, and Batman's getting old,
But you have your life in front of you, your future still to mound!

You could tackle modern slavery or rid some great disease,
Invent a new type of paper, that doesn't kill off trees.
You could make a difference, and might even come to find,
That you can save a life one day, just by being kind!

Even Superman has his faults, he's not all that he seems,
Society will be your Kryptonite, don't let them steal your dreams!

For now you're sleeping soundly, in your little bed,
With thoughts of capes and masks, running through your head.
Dream big and always know my son, there's no limit to what you'll be.
Because if it wasn't for you being who you are, then I would not be me!

M Y   H O P E S   F O R   Y O U

May you always grow up knowing everything you're worth.
How you have changed my life, just by being on this earth.
Never underestimate the value of being kind and true.
May someone's life be easier, because of what you do.
May you reach your full potential, dream big and then succeed.
May happiness and compassion drive the life you lead.
May adventure and discovery follow wherever you roam.
May you always know you're loved and find your way back home.

PICTURE PERFECT

Her life was picture perfect,
Because she never posted flaws.
We knew everything about her,
Except who she really was.
She could talk to 500 'friends'
Just by picking up her phone.
But was too afraid to tell them
She'd never felt so alone.
Everyone had their own life,
And it was perfect too!
But they hid behind their filters
And smiled inside their hue.
And maybe if she'd known
the truth behind their smile;
she might have changed her mind
Before deleting her profile.

IMPATIENT

I moaned throughout my pregnancy, I just couldn't wait for you.
And when you arrived two months early, I guessed you felt the same way too.
The guilt suddenly consumed me; I wanted to take back it all
As the highway of tubes and monitors helped your little chest rise and fall.
I just wanted to hold you; to comfort you with my touch.
You had been on this earth just moments and had already been through so much.
Now, I've never been a religious person but I prayed sincerely every second I could.
I believe hospital walls hear more genuine prayers than the walls of a church ever would.
I kept Virgil by your bedside, as you slept in your sterile dome
And I once again became so impatient, to have you healthy and home.
And as I think back on those moments, when I'm rocking you back to sleep.
I remember the deal that I made God, a promise that I had to keep.
"It will get easier when they get older." I would hear almost every day.
But I promised from that day forward, I'd never again wish your life away.

LAY BESIDE ME

Lay beside me mummy, cuddle me in tight.
Tell me another story, before we say goodnight.
Bedtime is my favourite, when we are all alone.
When the world has gone to sleep and we are on our own.

Stay with me a little longer, as I drift off to sleep;
Soon I'll be all grown up, but just now I'm your to keep.
So tell me that you love me and stroke my little head,
It won't be long until I'm too big for this bed.

Stay with me mummy, I know you've lots to do
But nothing is more important, than I am to you.
Lay beside me mummy, please don't rush away.
Tomorrow I'll be older than I was today.

And when I'm all grown up and have moved away from home,
You'll think back on this precious time that was ours alone.
So lay beside me mummy, and cuddle me in tight.
We don't know what tomorrow brings, but for now we have tonight.

A DAUGHTER'S POEM

This is for my daughter;
Some advice and a life lesson.
Who knew your little feet
Could leave such a big impression.

You are born into a world
That won't always treat you fair.
They'll judge you on your looks
Or the colour of your hair.

You see, the world is often shallow.
At least, that's how it seems
They judge you for your fashion
Or the size inside your jeans.

But believe me when I tell you,
Your beauty is not skin-deep.
And a lion should not be affected
By the opinion of the sheep.

Those who judge you by your looks
You'll soon come to find,
Are full of insecurities
With sad and narrow minds.

It's not that you're not beautiful,
You're like an angel, here on earth!
I just don't want you believing,
that is all your worth.

People will try and change you
and tell you what to think.
"Sugar and spice and all things nice,
dressed in frills and pink."

It's Daddy and My job to teach you,
And we'll do the best we can,
that you are every bit as equal,
as your fellow man!

We will act on your behalf
until you have a voice,
Then, we'll always support you
But you're free to make your choice!

You could be a scientist
Or a civil engineer.
Go down the pub with all your mates,
Hell, even have a beer!

You could be a soldier
Who knows what you'll become?
You could be a doctor!
Or, a teacher just like mum.

Some people just don't understand,
and it's really not complex;
Your future is not determined
by your gender or your sex!

So wear whatever you like
The same rule applies with toys!
Don't categorise creativity
Into 'Girls' or 'Boys'.

All that matters is that you're happy
and kind to all you meet!
Now go make an impression,
with your tiny little feet!

YOUR LEGACY

When your road has ended, and you've taken your final breath,
What legacy will you leave behind, to be remembered in your death?
Will they say you liked the finer things, and had holidays every year?
That your house was always spotless, and your windows always clear.
Will they talk about your jewellery, your watch and diamond rings?
How your house was always brimming, with the most exquisite things.
Will they talk about your weight or your wrinkles when you frown?
Do you think all that will matter, as they lower you down?
And if you think those things important, when you're no longer around,
You'll find you're just as shallow, as that hole dug in the ground.

LOST PROPERTY (PART 2)

It's easy to judge their mother,
When you only get a glance.
But her troubles stemmed from childhood;
She never stood a chance!

She was dragged up by her father,
Who was hardly ever there.
Her and her older sister,
had been in and out of care.

When her father lost his temper
He would result to using his fists.
He sister's coping mechanism,
was to take it out on her wrists.

One very violent evening,
As she cried herself to sleep,
Her sister couldn't take the pain anymore
And cut herself too deep.

When she found her in the morning,
She shut down from the pain.
She decided from that day forward,
She would never be hurt again!

She spent the rest of her youth
Living out on the street.
Revelling in the attention
From the men that she'd meet.

She soon moved in with a boyfriend;
He was abusive too!
Yet, somehow it made her feel better,
Because it was something that she knew.

They had two children together,
One girl then a little boy.
She adored every bone in their bodies;
They were her pride and joy!

And now when her partner turned violent
She was certain that it couldn't last
She'd damn sure not condemn her babies
To the same fate as her past.

So she took her precious children
And snuck out into the dark.
Found a modest place to live
And borrowed money from a shark.

They barely had essentials
But at least they were safe for now.
She tried to be a loving mother
But no one had shown her how.

The loan shark came out of the blue,
to cash in on unpaid debts.
He passed comments on her children,
making far from empty threats.

She needed more time to repay him;
They barely had enough to eat.
So he offered a dark alternative;
To work for him on the street.

She had no choice but to accept
She didn't know what else to do.
As she numbed her emotions with alcohol
Just to get her through.

She tried making it up to her babies,
She would save up all of her tips.
Then on the last Friday of every month,
she'd treat them to a big bag of chips.

She was plagued with guilt and regret
And apologised for being their mother.
The children told her they'd all be alright,
As long as they still had each other!

So they carried on together as family,
Despite the tragic cost.
Their bellies were empty but their hearts were full,
And without her, they would be lost.

YIN YANG

She was just happy to follow,
He was always the one in control.
She was as white as snowflakes,
he was as dark as coal.
She thought them the perfect couple,
She was the Yang, he was the Yin.
Together they were indestructible,
They could conquer anything.
But when their duo became a trio,
It stripped their powers bare.
Yin didn't realise Yang
Had more than enough love to share.
So Yin left them both one evening,
and vanished out into the night.
And when Yang awoke in the morning,
All that was left was her white.
So she took her new formed duo
And soon rebuilt her soul
And looking back she realised Yin
Was nothing but a black hole.

TEACH THE RIGHT LESSONS

There will be plenty of time to learn
But just now it's time to play.
Don't fixate on what your child will become,
And forget who they are today.

I'm glad you can hold a pencil,
I see you can write your name
But, did you ask that child, standing all alone
To come join in your game?

I see you aced your spelling test
And got full marks on your maths.
But, when that girl was struggling to read
Did you join in the laughs?

Did you share your lunchbox
With the kid that had no snack?
Did you hold out your hand
When that boy fell on his back?

When the teacher is doing her lesson.
Did you listen instead of talking?
Did you help that kid carry his bag?
Because he uses sticks for walking.

Did you say please and thank you?
Or, hold open the door?
I'm more interested in your manners
Than I am in your test score.

Of course I care about your education
And want you to succeed
But what good is being a genius
When you don't help those in need?

LITTLE DREAMER

Sleep well little dreamer.
Rest your weary head.
Your brain is making connections,
from the comfort of your bed.
It's putting together the pieces,
Of all the things you've seen,
Of all the words you've heard
And the places that you've been.
It's painting you a picture
Of all the things you know.
Your body needs its rest,
So that your mind can grow.
So, sleep well little dreamer
And file your thoughts away.
When you wake, you'll be even wiser
than you were before today.

THE FIRSTS AND THE LASTS

Don't you think it's funny, don't you think it's strange.
How the days and nights seem endless, and nothing seems to change?
Then one day you realise just how far you came,
And the realisation hits you, that nothing's stayed the same.
They say the days are long, but the years go by so fast.
You get so caught up on firsts that you forget about the lasts.
I was too busy toilet training to remember when I last changed your bum.
When did you stop calling me 'Mummy' and shorten it just to 'Mum'?
Then one day I put you down and I didn't realise it then,
You stopped wanting me to lift you, and never wanted carried again.
I was too busy straightening your tie and getting you ready for school.
I didn't notice you no longer kissed me, because it was no longer 'cool'.
And even now you're a teenager, you still keep me up late at night;
Waiting on you coming home from a party, just to be sure you're alright.
Now, years on from your childhood, I never thought I would find
That I missed those long days and nights, I couldn't wait to leave behind.
Now our sleepy night time cuddles are distant memories, in the past.
I was so excited about all of your firsts, that I forgot to savour our lasts.

TRAITS

There were traits that he was born with,
That he couldn't do much about.
His eye colour from his father,
And his mother's distinctive pout.
Yet, some things weren't inherited,
Unlike the blonde hair on his head,
They developed in his environment,
And were definitely not bred.
Like the hatred that he felt,
That came from deep within,
When he encountered another being
With a different colour of skin.
Or how he felt superior,
And thought he was above,
People that repulsed him,
Because of who they loved.
And all that 'education'
That had been fostered since his youth,
Had made him narrow- minded
And blind to the truth.
His privileged, middle class background,
He thought made him smart,
Was completely overshadowed
By the hatred in his heart!

LITTLE WANDERER

Go forth little wanderer
You have so much still to see.
Your feet will take you places
Your mind will set you free.
You're not made for this concrete jungle
Of offices and suits.
If man were meant to be stationary
Our legs would have been roots.
So go forth little wanderer
Live out your wildest dreams
You have wanderlust and adventure
In the fabric of your genes.

Printed in Great Britain
by Amazon